Beginning

STRENGTH TRAINING

The following athletes were photographed for this book:
Abdul Awad
Marc Bell
Bonne Chance
Heather Clark
Jeremy Cook
Moriah Cooperson
Cameron Darlington
Nick Fonville
James Goldsby
Deidre Golej
Koy Hardy
Jaspreet Kalsi
Chad Kim
David Lee
Myisha Love
Mona Montoya
Christina Muela
Matt Peck
Nate Sapington
Kim Schwarzkopf
Elizabeth Simas
Brian Sims
Sheri Sorensen
Melissa Tews
Fernando Trejo
Janie Villegas
Anne Williams

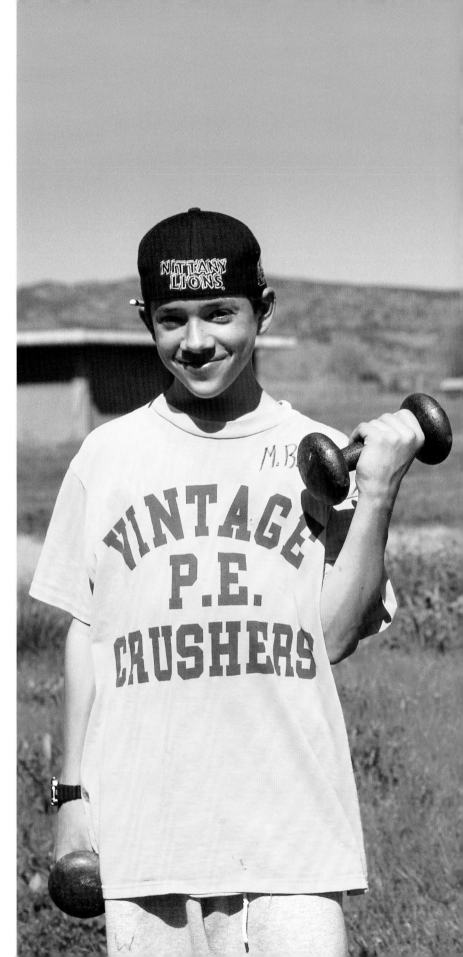

Beginning
STRENGTH TRAINING

Lori Coleman

Adapted from Jeff Savage's
Fundamental Strength Training
Photographs by Jimmy Clarke

Lerner Publications Company ● Minneapolis

The Beginning Sports series was designed in conjunction with the Fundamental Sports series to offer young athletes a basic understanding of various sports at two reading levels.

Photo Acknowledgments
Photos are reproduced with the permission of: Corbis-Bettmann, pp. 7, 8; UPI/Corbis-Bettmann, pp. 9 (top), 35 (top); Blank Archives/Archive Photos, p. 9 (bottom); Archive Photos, p. 10 (top); Gene Lester/Archive Photos, p. 10 (bottom); Stephen Downs/Archive Photos, p.11; © 1998/Nik Wheeler, p. 21; Reuters/Joe Giza/Archive Photos, p. 50; © ALLSPORT USA/Simon Bruty, p. 52; Reuters/Corbis-Bettmann, p. 55; SportsChrome East/West (David Lee Waite), p. 56 (left); © ALLSPORT USA/Bill Dobbins, p. 56 (right); © ALLSPORT USA/Doug Pensinger, p. 57 (both); © ALLSPORT USA/Rick Stewart, p. 58.
Artwork by Laura Westlund and John Erste.

Library of Congress Cataloging-in-Publication Data

Coleman, Lori.
   Beginning strength training / Lori Coleman, adapted from Jeff Savage's Fundamental strength training ; photographs by Jimmy Clarke.
     p. cm.
   Includes bibliographical references (p.) and index.
   Summary: Introduces the sport of strength training, including its history, terminology, workouts, and competitions.
   ISBN 0-8225-3511-4 (alk. paper)
   1. Weight training—Juvenile literature. 2. Bodybuilding—Juvenile literature. [1. Weight training.] I. Clarke, Jimmy, ill. II. Savage, Jeff, 1961– Fundamental strength training. III. Title.
GV546.C62 1998
613.7'13—dc21   97-51712

Manufactured in the United States of America
1 2 3 4 5 6 – JR – 04 03 02 01 00 99

Contents

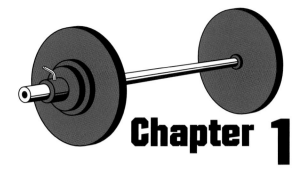

Chapter 1

How This Sport Got Started

Few people are natural athletes. Most of us have to work hard at sports. We can only do what our bodies let us do. One secret to success is improving our strength. Strength training—using weights, **resistance tools,** or simple exercises—makes muscles stronger. An athlete can train to build muscles and make the body more efficient. Strength training can help you run faster, jump higher, throw a ball harder, and hit or kick a ball farther. It shapes our bodies and makes us feel better about ourselves.

Strength training is safe for most people. Height, weight, and physical ability don't really matter. Strength training takes effort and dedication, and it teaches us patience.

Eugene Sandow

Eugene Sandow was a pioneer in American weight training. Sandow was an Englishman who performed great feats of strength in the 1890s. He first traveled across Europe as The Great Sandow. He raised men over his head and even lifted horses into the air.

Sandow soon came to the United States. He was called the World's Strongest Man and became an instant hit with fans. He would pose and flex his muscles in front of hundreds of admirers.

Strength Training's History

No one is sure when strength training began. In ancient times, men were honored for having muscular bodies. A popular sport in ancient Greece was stone lifting. Later people began competing to see who could lift the most weight.

In the late 1800s, strength contests were held in Europe. Men with large, beefy bodies usually won. In 1898, George Hackenschmidt won the Russian weight lifting championship. Hackenschmidt, nick-named the Russian Lion, had a lean, wiry body. After winning, the Russian Lion earned a fortune showing off his strength. He entertained people by lifting four or more men off the ground with one arm. He juggled 200-pound dumbbells while doing somersaults. Hackenschmidt was also a great runner, jumper, wrestler, and swimmer.

In 1903 Bernarr Macfadden, an American fitness buff, spon-sored a contest. The contest was held to select America's Most Perfectly Developed Man.

Bernarr Macfadden and his daughters flex their muscles during a 1925
radio broadcast.

Contestants were judged on muscle development. The contest became a popular yearly event. Angelo Siciliano won the contest in 1922. He decided he could make a fortune with his muscular body. First he changed his name to Charles Atlas. Then he designed a muscle-development program. He advertised the program in comic books and magazines. Millions of kids have seen the ad. It shows a skinny boy who gets sand kicked in his face by a bully. The boy takes the Charles Atlas course and returns to the beach to beat up the bully.

In 1939 the first Mr. America contest was held. Other contests such as Mr. Universe and Mr. Olympia soon followed. **Bodybuilding** became really popular when Steve Reeves won the Mr. America contest. Reeves lifted weights every day at a place called Muscle Beach in southern California. His charm made him famous. He started a movie career starring in *Hercules*.

Top, Steve Reeves at left happily poses at Muscle Beach with his costars in the movie *Athena*. Above, a crowd gathers around a new weight-lifting machine at Muscle Beach in 1956.

Arnold Schwarzenegger

In 1967 Arnold Schwarzenegger won the Mr. Universe contest. He moved to the United States from Austria. He, too, wanted to be a movie actor. Many young weight trainers admire Schwarzenegger for his dedication and for his build.

In the 1960s, many people still felt that weight training was bad for most athletes. People thought that bigger muscles made athletes less flexible. Vince Lombardi, coach of the Green Bay Packers football team, helped change that way of thinking. His football players began lifting weights. Then they won the first two Super Bowls, in 1967 and 1968. Soon all pro football players were lifting weights.

Bodybuilding contests for women began in the 1970s. Cory Everson, Sandy Riddell, and five-time Ms. Olympia Lenda Murray gained fame. But most women in other sports still stayed away from weights and strength training.

In the 1980s, athletes in sports such as baseball, golf, and tennis began to see that strength training could help them. They found that strength training improved their batting, hitting, and speed. They did not lose their touch or flexibility as they had feared. Instead they gained power and endurance.

Today most men's and women's sports teams do strength training. Many high schools offer classes on weight lifting. Some junior high school programs are also joining in. More than one million people in the United States do strength training.

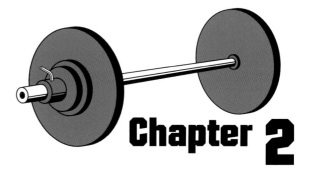

Chapter 2

BASICS

To do strength training, you will need the right equipment and a good place to work out. Health clubs are everywhere. Most of them have trainers who can teach proper technique. Many schools have weight rooms where students can work out. You can also strength train at home.

The two types of weights people use are **free weights** and **weight machines.** Free weights consist of bars and plates made of iron. A simple set of free weights has a long bar called a barbell, two short bars called dumbbells, and at least 100 pounds of assorted weights. Weight machines are usually found in health clubs. They are useful in exercising certain muscles, and they are fun to use.

Many basic lifts are done while sitting or lying on the weight bench. A weight bench is about as tall and wide as a picnic table bench but half as long. The bench you use should be padded and sturdy. Most weight benches can also be raised at an angle, or incline. The bench then becomes an **incline bench.**

Certain lifts can only be performed on machines. With machines, the weight slides along metal guides. The guides help steady the weight. Free weights must be balanced. Free weights are harder to handle, especially for beginners.

You should wear comfortable, loose-fitting clothes for weight training. Shorts and a T-shirt

Free Weight Equipment

It takes time to get to know the benches, barbells, dumbbells, pulleys, and other devices available in your weight room. Never be afraid to ask questions if you don't know how to use something. Most school and health club weight rooms have professional staff members who can help you. If you can't find help, stick to the basics—situps, pushups, chinups, and exercises using a regular bench, dumbbells, and a barbell.

are good. Athletic shoes are important for solid footing.

Getting Ready

Be sure to warm up and stretch before training with weights. Some beginners skip this and go straight to the weights. If you don't warm up and stretch, you could injure yourself.

Many weight lifters wear gloves to protect their hands. Gloves cushion the weight. Some weight lifters wear a heavy belt around their waist to support their lower back muscles. But beginners don't need a belt.

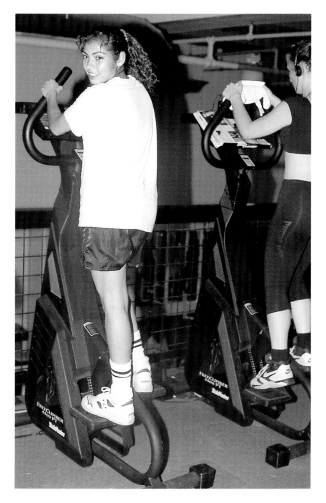

Christina warms up on a stair-climbing machine.

Warming up gets the oxygen in your blood to your muscles. Your muscles need oxygen to work. One way to warm up your muscles is to run for about 10 minutes. You can run around a track or on a tread-mill like Christina and Moriah. Anne rides on a stationary bike. Chad jumps rope.

Now that you have warmed up, you need to stretch your muscles. You should stretch both before and after strength training. Hold every stretch without bouncing. Bouncing can cause injury. When stretching leg muscles, do not lock your knees. That can also cause injury. Here are a few easy stretching exercises to do before and after your workout.

Shoulder shrugs loosen the upper back and shoulders. Marc stands with his feet apart. He raises both shoulders up toward his neck, like shrugging. Then he lowers them. Marc repeats this 10 times.

Triceps stretches loosen the muscles at the back side of the upper arm. David raises his left arm. He grasps his left elbow with his right hand. He pulls gently to the right until he feels the muscle stretching and holds it for 10 seconds. David repeats with the opposite arm.

Side bends stretch the sides of your body. Heather, Mona, Jaspreet, and Janie stand with their feet apart. They raise their right arms over their heads. They bend slowly down to the left. They hold this position for 20 seconds. They repeat the stretch on the opposite side.

Sky stretches stretch the upper back and the sides. Do sky stretches like side bends, but reach up.

Forward bends loosen your lower back and the backs of your legs. Jeff bends forward and reaches toward his feet. He keeps his knees slightly bent. He stretches for 30 seconds.

Quadriceps stretches are for the muscles at the front of your thighs. Kim reaches back and grabs her right ankle, pulling her foot up behind her. She stretches for 30 seconds. Then Kim stretches her other side.

Calf stretches are for the backs of your lower legs. Kim puts one foot in front of the other. She places both hands against a wall. She leans forward and keeps the heel of her back foot on the floor. Kim stretches for 20 seconds. Then she repeats the stretch with the other leg.

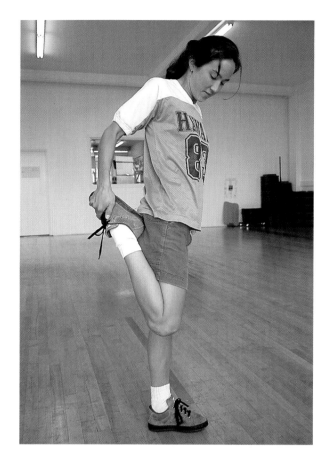

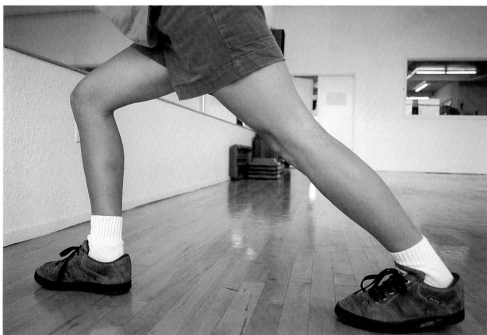

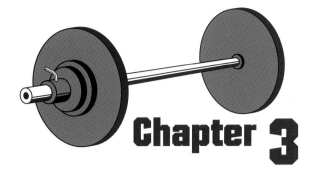

Chapter 3

THE LIFTS

Strength training can be done without weights. **Calisthenics** can be performed wherever you have enough room to do them. Pushups build chest muscles. Chinups build upper back muscles. Dips develop arm and chest muscles. Squats build leg muscles. Situps build stomach muscles. You will get a super workout and make great gains in strength by doing these exercises alone.

Many people also use free weights, resistance equipment, and weight machines. Resistance exercises can be done with a partner. Your partner provides the resistance as you push with different muscle groups. You can also use resistance equipment, such as a piece of rubber tubing. When strength training, remember the basic rules. Quit if it's hard to

Muscles

The human body has more than 600 muscles. Each muscle is made up of fiber. When you lift weight, you exercise some of the fiber. When muscle fibers are exercised, they break down. Muscles respond by repairing broken-down fibers and building them up bigger and stronger.

21

continue. Exhale, or breathe out, when lifting or pushing or pulling. Inhale, or breath in, when returning to the starting position. With situps, for example, exhale while raising your head and shoulders off the floor. Inhale on the way back down.

If using weights, remember, they are heavy! If you hold the plates the wrong way, you might end up with a smashed toe. You could wind up with an injured back if you load the plates onto the barbell the wrong way. There are a couple simple safety rules. One, always use both hands when holding plates. Two, always bend your knees when lifting plates from the floor and loading them onto the bar. Once you've slipped the plates onto the bar, fasten the collars with their locking screws. Weights must be handled with care.

Six main body areas are exercised in strength training: chest, back, shoulders, arms, abdomen, and legs. There are some basic lifts for each area. You can use the following exercises in a program like the one shown in chapter 4.

Human Muscular System

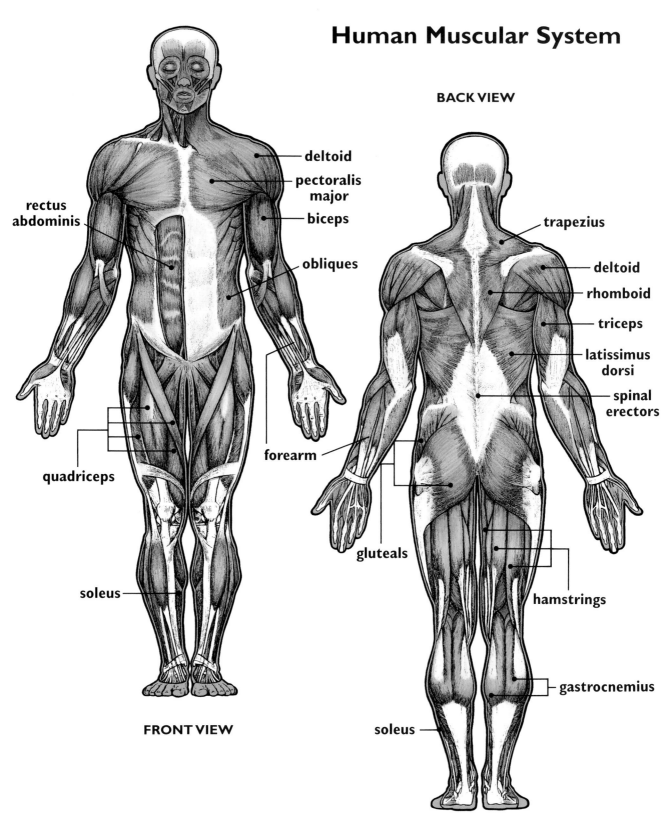

BACK VIEW

deltoid

pectoralis major

biceps

rectus abdominis

obliques

trapezius

deltoid

rhomboid

triceps

latissimus dorsi

spinal erectors

quadriceps

forearm

gluteals

hamstrings

soleus

gastrocnemius

soleus

FRONT VIEW

Chest

The main chest muscles are the pectorals (pecs). Pecs are used to push and punch.

● *Bench Press*

The bench press is for the pecs. Brian lies on the bench. He plants his feet firmly on the floor for balance. He lifts the bar off the rack. He holds it at arm's length, just short of locking his elbows. Then Brian lowers the bar to his chest and pauses. He keeps his elbows out to the sides. Then Brian presses the bar upward. He stops just before his elbows lock. That completes one **repetition,** or rep.

Moriah completes some reps on a bench press machine.

● Incline Bench Press

Incline bench presses are for the upper pectorals. Moriah lies back on the incline bench with her feet on the floor. She lifts the bar off the rack and holds it up. Moriah then lowers the bar slowly. She touches the bar gently to her chest, stopping for a moment. She then presses it back up to the starting position. Like Moriah, be careful to balance the bar in this exercise.

Bench presses and incline bench presses also can be done with dumbbells. James holds the dumbbells with his palms facing forward. He does the dumbbell presses the same way as barbell presses are done.

● *Fly*

Flys are another type of chest lift that exercises the pectoral muscles. Nick lies on the bench just like he would for presses. He holds a dumbbell in each hand. With the palms facing each other, he holds the dumbbells up above his chest.

Nick lowers the dumbbells out and down to either side in a wide arc. He stops when the weights reach below shoulder level. He is careful to keep his elbows bent slightly and the weight steady. Slowly Nick lifts the weight back upward through the arc, as if giving someone a big bear hug. Nick returns the dumbbells to the starting position.

Flys can be performed on machines as well. Fly machines are sometimes called "pec decks." When doing machine flys, Moriah keeps her feet on the floor. Her back is against the back rest.

Back

The important muscles of the back are the trapezius, latissimus dorsi, rhomboids, and spinal erectors. The trapezius (traps) is a triangular muscle. It extends from the neck to the shoulder blades. The latissimus dorsi (lats) are large triangle-shaped muscles. They extend from the shoulders to the lower back. The lats are the largest muscles of the upper body. They work to pull the arms back. The rhomboids are between the traps and lats. The spinal erectors are in the lower back. They hold the spine up straight.

● *Traps*

Dumbbell shrugs and upright rows develop the traps. Marc does dumbbell shrugs. He holds dumbbells down at his sides. Keeping his arms straight, Marc raises his shoulders up until he feels a squeeze. He holds it for a moment, then returns to the starting position. He tries not to move anything but his shoulders.

Upright rows are done with the barbell. Kim holds the bar with an overhand grip. She lifts the bar to her chin. She holds it there for a split-second and then lowers it.

● Lats

Chinups mainly develop the lat muscles. Kim grabs the chinning bar with an underhand grip. She hangs from the bar, then pulls herself up until her chin reaches the bar. Then Kim lowers herself to the starting position.

You must lift your entire body weight to do a chinup. If you cannot, a lat machine is useful. A lat machine lets you do the chinup movement with less weight.

● Lower Back

Rows are great for the lower back muscles. You need a dumbbell and a bench to do one-arm dumbbell rows. Melissa puts her right knee and right hand on the bench. She pulls the dumbbell up with her left hand, keeping her body steady. She pauses at the top. Then she lowers the dumbbell.

Seated cable rows are done on a machine. Moriah and Anne sit with their feet braced against the crossbar. They grab the handles and pull them in. They pause and then let the handles go forward again.

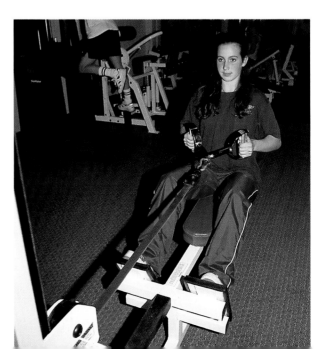

Shoulders

Deltoids are the main shoulder muscles. Each arm has front deltoids, middle deltoids, and rear deltoids. The deltoids help raise the upper arm.

● *Front Deltoids*

Military presses develop the front deltoids. Myisha holds the bar in front of her chest with a wide overhand grip. Myisha lifts the bar straight over her head. She then lowers the bar.

Spotter

A spotter helps guide the movement of the weights. The spotter is ready to help you if the weight begins to slip from your grip or becomes too heavy for you to lift. The spotter encourages you to complete sets and train hard.

Arnolds are named for Arnold Schwarzenegger. Koy holds two dumbbells at shoulder height. Her palms face in. Koy lifts the dumbbells over her head. At the same time, she turns them to face out. She then lowers the weights and twists them back in.

● *Middle Deltoids*

Behind-the-head presses use the middle deltoids. Kim holds the bar behind her head with a wide overhand grip. She keeps her elbows back. She lifts the bar straight up. Kim then carefully lowers the weight.

● *Rear Deltoids*

Lateral raises work the rear deltoids. Sheri, Jaspreet, and Janie stand with their feet apart. With a dumbbell in each hand, they bend forward. With palms facing down, they lift the weights up and out to the side. Then they slowly lower them.

Arms

The biceps is at the front of the upper arm. People often flex this muscle to show their strength. The triceps is at the back of the arm. The forearm group of muscles encircles the arm between the elbow and wrist. These muscles move the hand up and down.

● *Biceps*

Curls develop the biceps. For standing barbell curls, Fernando stands with his feet apart and his knees bent slightly. He holds the bar with an under-hand grip. Fernando pulls the bar up and in a wide arc toward his neck. Then he lowers the weight to the starting position.

Handicapped Lifters

Many different people with handicaps or disabilities do strength training exercises. They benefit from them the same as everyone else. Specially challenged kids can do situps, pushups, chinups, and all the lifts. Having a spotter around for help and support makes lifting fun and safe for people with handicaps.

Arnold Schwarzenegger coaches a Special Olympics weight training program.

Jeremy holds a dumbbell in each hand to do alternate dumbbell curls. His palms face in. He curls his right hand out and up to the right shoulder. He turns his palm toward the shoulder. He keeps his elbow close to his side. Jeremy lowers his right hand at the same time he curls his left hand up to the left shoulder.

● *Triceps*

Triceps are strengthened with extensions and cable pressdowns. To do extensions, lie on your back on the bench. Keep your knees bent and your feet flat on the bench. Fernando holds the barbell in an overhand grip. His hands are about 10 inches apart. He presses the barbell up above his head but does not lock his elbows. Fernando keeps his elbows in. He slowly lowers the barbell to just above his forehead. Extensions can also be done one arm at a time with a single dumbbell.

To do cable pressdowns, you will need a pulley. On one end of the pulley is the weight. On the other end is a short bar. The pulley has a cable that moves up over a wheel and back down to the bar. Deidre holds the short bar with both hands in an overhand grip. Deidre presses the bar down but doesn't lock her elbows. She lets the bar come back up until her arms are parallel to the floor. Throughout the motion she keeps her elbows in.

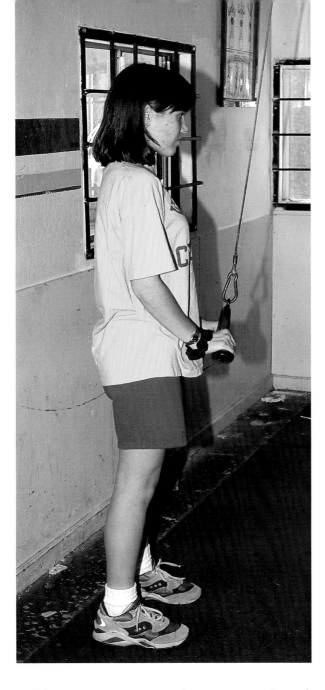

Forearms can be exercised with wrist curls. Kim holds a dumbbell and rests her forearm on her thigh. She moves her wrist forward, lowering the dumbbell slightly. Then she bends her wrist back to raise the bar up. The bar only moves a few inches in each direction. Kim repeats with the other arm.

Abdomen

The main abdominal muscles are the rectus abdominis (abs) and the external obliques. The abs extend from the lower chest to the hips. The obliques are on each side. They bend, rotate, and turn the body.

● Abs

Situps work your upper abs. Leg raises develop your lower abs. For situps, Kim lies on a mat. She clasps her hands behind her neck. She bends her knees and keeps her feet flat on the floor. You may tuck your feet under a support or have a partner hold them down. Kim slowly raises her upper torso a few inches off the floor. She

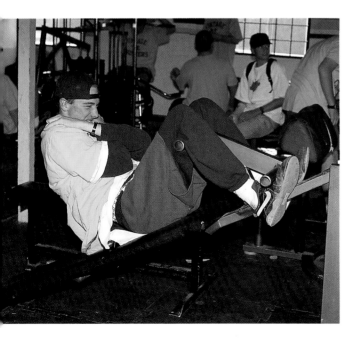

change is that your head is lower than your feet. That makes the situps harder to do.

Twisting situps are another type of situps. Kim twists slightly to one side as she nears the top of the situp. She points her elbow at the opposite knee. Next time she rises and points the other elbow at the opposite knee.

Kim lies on a mat for leg raises. Her hands are down at her sides. She slowly raises her legs straight up without bending at the knees. Kim holds her legs for a moment about two feet from the ground. Then she slowly lowers them to the mat.

pauses, then slowly returns to the floor. Do not sit up all the way to your knees. To protect your back, be careful not to jerk your body up.

Incline board situps are done almost the same way. The

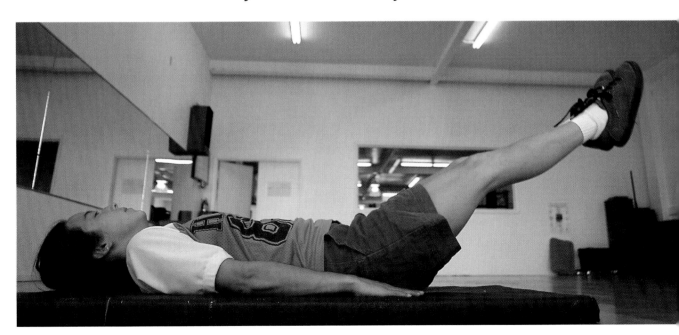

● *Obliques*

Side leg raises work your obliques. Kim lies on her side. She lifts her top leg as high as she can. Then she lowers it.

Crunches are great for the entire abdomen. Abdul and James lie on their backs. Their hands are clasped behind their heads. Their knees are bent. They begin, lifting the head and shoulders toward the knees. At the same time, they pull the knees in toward the shoulders.

Legs

The quadriceps, gluteals, hamstring, soleus, and gastrocnemius are the main leg muscles. The quadriceps (quads) are at the front of the thigh. The quads move the lower leg at the knee. The gluteals (glutes) form the rear end. The glutes push the upper leg backward. The hamstring at the back of the thigh bends the leg up and back. The soleus and gastrocnemius muscles are in the lower leg. They provide power when jumping and running.

Squats are good overall leg exercises. To do squats, Abdul balances a barbell across his shoulders. Abdul slowly lowers to the ground in a squat position. He keeps his head up and back straight. Then he pushes himself back up.

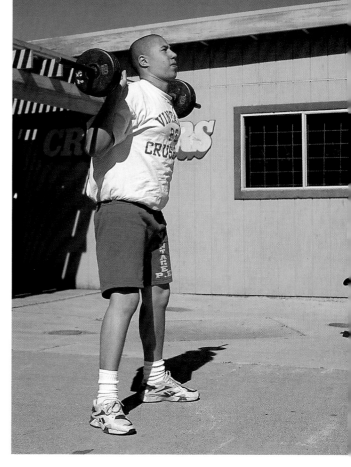

To do a lunge, step forward as you lower the weight. The knee of your back leg should almost touch the floor.

Leg presses are done on a machine. Jeremy sits with his feet on the platform. He pushes against the weight, straightening his legs but not locking his knees. Then he bends his knees, lowering the weight.

Leg curls work the hamstrings. Anne lies face down on the leg curl machine. She places her heels under the curl bar. She pulls the bar up and in toward her body. Slowly Anne then lowers it back down.

Standing calf raises develop the calf muscles. Matt stands on the balls of his feet on a block of wood. He balances a barbell across his shoulders. He bends his knees slightly. Matt lowers his heels as far as he can. Then he raises up.

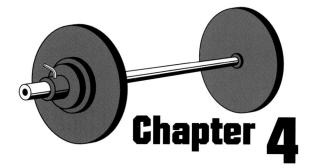

Chapter 4

WORKOUT

Once you have learned about strength training exercises, you may want to begin doing them. But which exercises should you do? How often should you do them? How much weight should you use?

To develop your muscles, you must do each exercise a number of times. Each time you do a situp or chinup or lift a weight, you have done a repetition (rep). A series of reps (about 8 and 12) is a **set.** You should do at least one set but not more than five. A series of

different lifts is a **workout routine.** A sequence of workout routines is a **program.**

Use a weight that is comfortable for doing at least 8 reps. You shouldn't be able to do more than 12. If you cannot do 8 reps, use less weight. Add a little more weight if you can do more than 12 reps. The last few reps of a set should be harder to do. Rest for at least one minute between sets. This is the amount of time your body needs for blood to flush through the muscle. The

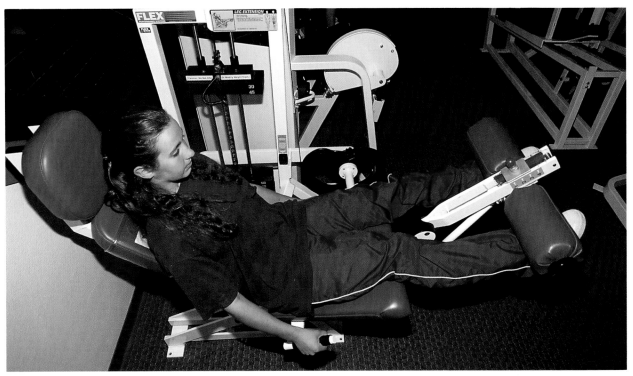

Anne works out on the leg extension machine.

blood removes waste that is created as the muscle works. It also gives the muscle energy.

Athletes working for better endurance and muscle tone should lift less weight and do more reps. This type of lifting is best for young athletes. Lifters who want bigger muscles lift more weight and do fewer reps. This type of lifting is not good for young athletes.

Once you finish your workout, your muscles need to rest. Muscles need time to recover and grow. Working the same muscles every day will not make them grow faster. Working out every day can tear your muscles and slow their growth. It is best not to exercise the same muscles two days in a row. Muscles actually grow while resting.

On the next two pages is a simple training program. This guide shows workouts three days a week—Monday, Wednesday, and Friday. You can design your own workout program and choose your own workout days. But be sure you give your muscles at least a day of rest between workouts.

Nutrition

Proper nutrition is always important, but it is key when weight training. Exercising takes energy, which comes from a single source—food. Without the right food in your body, you will not have the energy to exercise.

You've probably heard the phrase "well-balanced diet." This is what you need to eat to perform in the weight room. What exactly is meant by well balanced? It means a proper mix of proteins, carbohydrates, fats, minerals, vitamins, and water.

Protein comes mainly from fish, chicken and other meats, eggs, and beans. The body uses protein to create muscle tissue. Without enough protein, muscles will not grow.

Carbohydrates come mostly from potatoes, pasta, tortillas, rice, and other grains, vegetables, and fruits. Carbohydrates provide the energy needed to exercise.

Fats are found in many foods and are important in small quantities. Fat supplies the body with a cushion to protect the heart and other organs. But too much fat is unhealthy.

A common myth in weight training is the more you eat, the more your muscles will grow. But if you eat a lot of food, most of it will be stored as fat.

The correct rule is this—eat a well-balanced diet and train hard, and you will see your body grow stronger.

Bench presses

MONDAY

Chest

bench dumbbell presses   3 sets
incline bench dumbbell
  presses   3 sets
flys   4 sets

Triceps

extensions   4 sets
cable pressdowns   4 sets

Abdomen

situps   30 reps
incline board situps   20 reps

WEDNESDAY

Back

dumbbell shrugs   4 sets
upright barbell rows   3 sets
chinups (or lats)   4 sets
one-arm dumbbell rows   4 sets

Biceps/Forearm

standing barbell curls   4 sets
alternate dumbbell curls   3 sets
wrist curls   3 sets

Abdomen

twisting situps   25 reps
leg raises   25 reps

FRIDAY

Shoulders

Arnolds	3 sets
behind-the-back presses	4 sets
lateral raises	3 sets

Legs

squats (or lunges)	4 sets
leg presses	4 sets
leg curls	4 sets
standing calf raises	3 sets

Abdomen

side leg raises	30 reps
crunches	35 reps

Leg curls

Standing barbell curls

Training Right

Many lifters, especially beginners, try to lift more weight than they can handle. This can cause lots of problems without doing anything to improve strength. Perfect form and technique are key in strength training. Cheating to lift more weight or to do more repetitions, like swaying your back to do a few more arm curls, can cause an injury. If you cheat on a lift, you are not exercising the intended muscle. You are also risking a problem that could keep you from training. Never be embarrassed about the amount of weight you can lift. If you are training, you are improving. And if you do the lifts with good technique, you will get stronger.

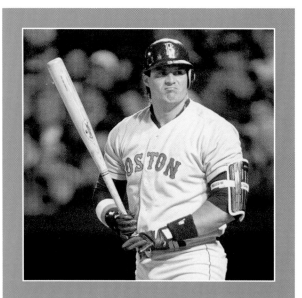

Jose Canseco

Slugger Jose Canseco credits his great success in baseball to weight training. Jose was not picked until the 15th round of the baseball draft in 1982 by the Oakland A's. He wasn't expected to do much. For a few years in the minors he didn't.

Then Jose began lifting weights with A's strength coach Dave McKay. By 1986, Jose was bigger, stronger, and faster. He made the A's major league team. He belted 33 homers to win Rookie of the Year honors.

By 1988, Jose had packed on 40 pounds of muscle. That year he became the first player in history to hit 40 home runs and steal 40 bases in the same season. He was named baseball's Most Valuable Player.

Jose spends two hours a day in the weight room. He works on doing each exercise the right way. Coach McKay says, "Jose will never cheat on a lift. He will do it with perfect form and technique."

Not long ago, many coaches of various sports urged athletes to avoid strength training. They feared that lifting weights made athletes bulky, stiff, and slower. This idea is wrong. Athletes can get stronger without losing flexibility or speed. When competitors of equal skill are matched up, the stronger one usually triumphs. It is rare to find a pro athlete who does not do any strength training.

Many athletes do lifts to exercise the muscles they use in their sport. Downhill skier Picabo Street, for example, does a lot of lifts for her legs. Football linebacker Junior Seau works on his upper body strength. Swimmer Janet Evans lifts weights for her arms.

Sports and the lifts that help you do your best at each one:

	Baseball	Basketball	Biking	Football	Golf	Gymnastics	Hockey	Soccer	Softball	Skiing	Swimming	Tennis	Track and Field	Volleyball	Wrestling
bench presses	✓		✓	✓			✓	✓	✓				✓	✓	✓
flys			✓			✓					✓	✓		✓	
shrugs				✓		✓									✓
upright rows			✓	✓		✓				✓	✓		✓		✓
chinups		✓	✓	✓		✓				✓	✓	✓	✓		✓
rows			✓									✓			
military presses		✓		✓				✓							✓
Arnolds		✓		✓							✓				✓
lateral raises		✓			✓	✓						✓			
cable pressdowns	✓	✓							✓		✓	✓		✓	✓
wrist curls	✓		✓		✓		✓		✓			✓		✓	
abdominal exercises						✓		✓		✓	✓	✓	✓	✓	✓
squats	✓	✓	✓	✓	✓	✓	✓	✓	✓	✓					✓
lunges	✓			✓	✓		✓	✓	✓	✓					✓
leg presses				✓		✓		✓		✓	✓	✓	✓	✓	
leg curls							✓	✓		✓		✓	✓		
standing calf raises		✓		✓		✓	✓	✓				✓	✓	✓	

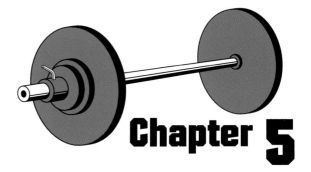

Chapter 5

COMPETITION

Strength training is mainly a competition with yourself. It helps you improve your body's fitness, power, and endurance. Competing against others at a young age is not a good idea. Growing bodies are more likely to get hurt under stress. Too much training can cause weight loss and soreness that won't go away. It can also make it easier for you to get sick. But experienced professional and amateur lifters do compete against each other.

There are three groups of professional weight lifters. They are **Olympic lifters, power lifters,** and bodybuilders. Anyone can be a professional weight lifter. Becoming a champion takes years of patience and dedication.

Steroids

Steroids are chemicals that affect growth. They also affect body tissues, reproduction, and behavior. Some professional bodybuilders take steroids to build their muscles. Taking them is cheating. Judges at most bodybuilding competitions do not test for steroids.

Some beginning and intermediate weightlifters believe they can get bigger muscles by taking steroids. This is false. Steroids do not necessarily build bigger muscles. Steroids can cause serious and permanent damage to your body. Abuse of steroids leads to headaches, nose bleeds, dizziness, acne, hair loss, high blood pressure, blood clots, liver cancer, and death. Steroids are illegal, dangerous drugs.

Power lifting

Power lifting competitions involve three lifts. These are the bench press, the squat, and the dead lift. The bench press and the squat are lifts we have already discussed. The third lift, the dead lift, is done by lifting the barbell from the floor to a standing position. The lifter uses mostly the thigh and back muscles. He or she crouches down and grabs the bar with one palm facing outward and the other facing inward. The lifter stands up with the bar. In all three lifts, the weight must be moving up steadily. If the weight stops moving, a red light flashes and the lift is not counted.

Power lifters compete year round in tournaments. There are several weight classes in which lifters are grouped according to weight. The person in each weight class who lifts the most weight combined in all three lifts is declared the winner of the weight class.

Bodybuilding

Like power lifters, bodybuilders compete in tournaments. Mr. America and Mr. Universe are two of these competitions. Bodybuilders do not lift weight during the competition. They are judged on how well their muscles are developed. They stand on a stage and flex their muscles for the judges. Posing is very important.

Bodybuilders spend most of the year lifting heavy weights. They gain as much muscle mass as possible. They also follow a strict low-fat diet plan. While they are training, body-builders do not look like they

Achim Albrecht, winner of the Mr. Universe title in 1990, poses with his medal.

do in magazines or on stage. They pace their workouts so that they peak at the right time for competitions.

Bodybuilders must be aware of every bite of food they take. They often become nutrition

Lenda Murray wins the Ms. Olympia title.

Many women enter bodybuilding contests.

experts as well as weight lifters. Several weeks before a competition, bodybuilders alter their diets to trim excess body fat. Less body fat makes muscles look more defined or "ripped." It takes many years of hard work to do well in bodybuilding competitions.

Olympic lifting

Olympic lifting involves two lifts—the clean and jerk and the snatch. The barbell is used for both lifts. The clean and jerk is a lift with two parts. First, the lifter raises the barbell from the floor to the chest. The lifter is squatting. He holds the barbell with an overhand grip. Then he pulls the bar upward from the floor as in an upright row. At the same time, the lifter stands straight up. The second part of the lift is lifting the barbell over the head. The lifter jumps and spreads his legs to help push up.

The snatch is done by lifting the barbell from the floor to overhead in one movement. The lifter uses a wide overhand grip. He bends at the knees and lifts the bar to waist level. He squats low beneath the bar and stands up. This is all in one motion. Both the clean and jerk and the snatch require quickness and good technique.

Olympic lifters compete in tournaments each year, including the world championships. They all hope to qualify for the ultimate meet held every four

Pablo Lara of Cuba, performing the snatch lift, won a gold medal at the 1996 Olympic Games.

years—the summer Olympic Games. Olympic lifting has been a part of the Olympics since the original modern Olympic Games in 1896. At the 1996 summer Olympics, 240 athletes from over 80 countries competed in weightlifting.

The first round of Olympic lifting is held the first 10 days of the Games. There are 10 weight classes. They range from 119 pounds to 238 pounds-and-over. In the Olympics, one weight class competes each day. The top finishers in each weight class advance to the final round. This is held the final two days of the Games. The winning lifters are based on the combined weights of their two lifts. One competitor from each class wins.

In both rounds of competition, each lifter gets three chances to lift as much weight as possible in the clean and jerk. Then the competitors get three chances at the snatch. The highest weights for each of the two lifts are combined. A lifter who fails at all three attempts in either of the lifts scores a zero for that lift.

Robin Goad

Robin Goad has won every big weightlifting competition in the world except the Olympics. That's because there is no women's Olympic weight-lifting event (yet). Robin is a teacher in Sumner, Washington. When she's not in the classroom, Robin usually is at Coffee's Gym, training with weights.

Robin stands 5 feet and weighs 110 pounds. But she has won the clean and jerk and snatch national championships eight times through 1996 and has five Olympic Festival gold medals.

In 1994, Robin broke a world record in the snatch. She lifted 181 3/4 pounds at the World Championships. She won her first world title that day. In 1995, Robin was a finalist for the Women's Sports Foundation SportsWoman of the Year. She has been honored three times as the U.S. Weightlifting Federation's Female Athlete of the Year.

No Olympic lifting competition for women has taken place yet. The International Olympic Committee plans to feature the first clean and jerk and snatch competitions for women at the 2000 Olympic Games in Sydney, Australia.

Power lifting World Records

SQUAT	Weight Lifted	Name	Body Weight	Nationality	Date of Lift
Men	1,003 lbs.	Kirk Karwoski	276 lbs.	USA	7-23-97
	837 lbs.	Mike Bridges	182 lbs.	USA	7-10-82
	612 lbs.	Andrzej Stanaszek	115 lbs.	Poland	8-10-97
Junior Men	987 lbs.	Shane Hamman	276+ lbs.	USA	7-31-94
	757 lbs.	Pat Roche	182 lbs.	USA	7-27-91
	573 lbs.	Chun-Hsiung Hu	123 lbs.	TPE	8-10-97
Women	612 lbs.	Juanita Trujillo	198+ lbs.	USA	7-31-94
	540 lbs.	Anne Sigrid Stiklestad	165 lbs.	Norway	6-20-97
	377 lbs.	Raija Koskinen	106 lbs.	Finland	8-9-97
Junior Women	584 lbs.	Chia-Sui Lee	198+ lbs.	TPE	8-9-97
	474 lbs.	Valida Iskandarova	149 lbs.	Kazakhstan	6-20-97
	336 lbs.	Svetlana Tesleva	97 lbs.	Russia	12-6-96

BENCH PRESS	Weight Lifted	Name	Body Weight	Nationality	Date of Lift
Men	711 lbs.	James Henderson	276+ lbs.	USA	7-13-97
	442 lbs.	Alexei Sivokon	149 lbs.	Kazakhstan	8-10-97
	413 lbs.	Magnus Carlsson	123 lbs.	Sweden	11-14-96
Junior Men	557 lbs.	Daisuke Midote	276 lbs.	Japan	7-9-95
	474 lbs.	Jan Germanus	182 lbs.	SLK	6-24-94
	391 lbs.	Andrzej Stanaszek	115 lbs.	Poland	11-16-94
Women	386 lbs.	Chen-Yeh Chao	198+ lbs.	TPE	8-9-97
	259 lbs.	Carrie Boudreau	123 lbs.	USA	8-9-97
	187 lbs.	Svetlana Tesleva	97 lbs.	Russia	12-6-96
Junior Women	342 lbs.	Natalia Payusova	198 lbs.	Russia	8-9-97
	321 lbs.	Marina Zhguleva	165 lbs.	Russia	6-20-97
	212 lbs.	Irina Krylova	106 lbs.	Russia	9-14-95

DEAD LIFT	Weight Lifted	Name	Body Weight	Nationality	Date of Lift
Men	895 lbs.	Lars Noren	276+ lbs.	Sweden	4-10-88
	744 lbs.	Dan Austin	165 lbs.	USA	7-30-94
	564 lbs.	E. S. Bhaskaran	115 lbs.	India	12-1-93
Junior Men	794 lbs.	Aarre Kapyla	205 lbs.	Finland	9-19-87
	740 lbs.	Sahroni	165 lbs.	INA	9-20-94
	535 lbs.	Dennis Thios	115 lbs.	INA	9-2-90
Women	579 lbs.	Katrina Robertson	198+ lbs.	Austria	6-21-97
	538 lbs.	Ruth Shafer	149 lbs.	USA	5-20-84
	364 lbs.	Nancy Belliveau	97 lbs.	USA	6-1-85
Junior Women	557 lbs.	Elena Suchoruk	165 lbs.	Ukraine	5-6-95
	419 lbs.	Oksana Belova	115 lbs.	Russia	6-27-96
	346 lbs.	Svetlana Tesleva	97 lbs.	Russia	12-6-96

The above records are a selection of weight class record holders. The top weight lifted in each class is the world record for that lift in that class. This information was compiled using data from the International Powerlifting Federation and the United States Weightlifting Federation.

STRENGTH TRAINING TALK

bodybuilding: A form of competition in which men and women pose to show judges their muscular development. The competitors are judged on the size, shape, definition of their muscles, which they develop through strength training.

calisthenics: Strength training exercises that use the body as resistance. Examples of calisthenic exercises are situps, pushups, crunches, side leg raises, dips, and pullups.

free weights: Barbells, dumbbells, and other equipment onto which weight plates can be loaded. A barbell is a long bar onto each end of which plates of varying weights can be loaded. Dumbbells are shorter bars that are usually used in pairs, one in each hand. Some dumbbells are simple bars onto which weights can be loaded, much like a barbell. Other dumbbells are weighted permanently with specific amounts of weight. For example, a set of dumbbells might consist of two 5-pound dumbbells, two 10-pound dumbbells, and two 15-pound dumbbells.

incline bench: A bench used with free weights that is set at an upward angle, typically about 45 degrees.

Olympic lifting: A form of competition in which participants attempt two lifts—the snatch and the clean and jerk. Each athlete gets three tries at each lift. For the snatch, the lifter must lift the barbell from the floor to overhead in one continuous movement. The clean and jerk consists of two motions—first the lifter raises the barbell to chest height and then raises it overhead as he or she stands. The best score for each lift is recorded, and the two scores are added for a total score.

power lifting: A form of competition in which the lifters get three tries each at the squat, the bench press, and the dead lift. For the squat, the lifter begins with the barbell across the back of the shoulders, then lowers the body by bending the knees until the thighs are parallel to the ground. For the bench press, the lifter lies on a bench facing up and lifts the barbell straight up from the chest. The lifter is in a standing position for the dead lift, grasping the barbell with one hand in an overhand grip and the other in an underhand grip. The barbell is lifted up from the ground as the lifter stands. The best score is taken for each lift. The three scores are added for a total score.

program: A long-term series of workout routines designed to work specific parts of the body on alternating days.

repetition: The completion of a single lift or exercise, such as one chinup, one bench press, or one squat.

resistance tools: Equipment for performing strength-training exercises without the use of weights. Rubber tubing is the most common resistance tool.

set: A series of repetitions of the same exercise. For example, a series of 10 consecutive Arnolds or 15 consecutive situps is a set. Normally, 1 to 4 sets of an exercise are done at a time.

weight machines: Machines equipped with weights for performing specific lifts. Nautilus, Universal, and Hydra-Gym weight machines use variable resistance, which means they provide maximum resistance at the lifter's strongest position in the lift and ease up on resistance at the point of least strength. Cybex, Biodex, and Lido equipment perform in a similar way but also control the speed at which the weight is lifted.

workout routine: An organized grouping of sets that work several different parts of the body. For example, a workout routine could consist of 1 to 3 sets each of leg presses, squats, calf raises, situps, Arnolds, and bench presses.

FURTHER READING

Roberts, Scott and Ben Weider. *Strength and Weight Training for Young Athletes.* Chicago: Contemporary Books, 1994.

Smith, Tim. *Youth Strength Training.* North Palm Beach, Florida: The Athletic Institute, 1988.

Seidler, Todd L. and Debra L. Waters and Wendy L. Wilson. *Weight Training and Fitness for Health and Performance.* Dubuque, Iowa: Kendall/Hunt Publishing Company, 1990.

FOR MORE INFORMATION

Strength of America, Inc.
P. O. Box 31447
Mesa, AZ 85275-1447

National Youth Sports Foundation
10 Meredith Circle
Needham, MA 02192

National Strength and Conditioning
    Association
P. O. Box 81410
Lincoln, NE 68501

Amateur Bodybuilding Association
Gold's Gym
1307 W 6th Street
Corona, CA 91720

U. S. Powerlifting Federation, Inc.
P. O. Box 2170
Kilgore, TX 75663

U. S. Weightlifting Federation
One Olympic Plaza
Colorado Springs, CO 80909

INDEX